SPILL SOME NEW BRIGHTNESS

Also by

Francine Marie Tolf

Spill Some
New Brightness

POEMS BY

FRANCINE MARIE TOLF

PINYON PUBLISHING
Montrose, Colorado

Cover Art: Ink and Alcohol Painting

Photo 236519548 © Rudchenko | Dreamstime.com

Photograph of Francine Marie Tolf by Marc Marcovitz

First Edition: April 2022

Pinyon Publishing
23847 V66 Trail, Montrose, CO 81403
www.pinyon-publishing.com

Library of Congress Control Number: 2022933685
ISBN: 978-1-936671-80-9

ACKNOWLEDGMENTS

The Christian Century: "On the Way to Work"; "Transfiguration in North Minneapolis"

Damselfly Press: "Mystery upon Mystery"

Dappled Things: "Chrysanthemum Leaves"

5 AM: "Billy Ray"; "The #17 Westbound"

Flint Hills Review: "The Theme Was Memory"

Freshwater Review: "Before Soldiers Shot Ana"

Gratefulness.org: "Lilly"

Imitation Fruit Journal: "The Bus Stop at Lake and France"

The Listening Eye: "Mortals and Immortals"

Plainsongs: "Words Meant to Wound"

Potpourri: "Workshop"

Santa Fe Literary Review: "For Matthew, Who Will Not Remember Me"

Spiritus: "Yes"

Under Purple Skies, ed. Frank Bures, Belt Publishing, 2019: "On 2nd Street NE"

A small number of poems appeared in *The Rough Edge of Joy*, published by Red Bird Chapbooks in 2016.

CONTENTS

THE CROSS-DRESSER IN AISLE SIX OF RAINBOW FOODS

I told myself I was done writing poetry.
Spent. I didn't miss it, either.
I knew the pool that once brimmed with images
would spill some new brightness.
I'd find a hobby that did not break my heart
again and again.
I told myself.
Then *she* had to strut past me
with her size twelve go-go boots
and her cheerleading skirt,
those thick, muscled calves, that platinum wig!
Over six foot tall yet vulnerable
to the worst kind of hate.
Pushing a cart loaded with Doritos and ice cream.
Making courage look easy.

LILLY

At fifty-three, I sometimes feel a subtle but irreversible sadness
seeping into my blood. I have failed at important things.
I long for a home I could love.

But recently, I brought into my thin-walled apartment a young cat
who is not at all sad. If a goddess had held this stray by the heel
and dipped her in brightness, as the infant Achilles was dipped,
she could not be more golden, the gold of a jar of marmalade
quivering in sun.

Sometimes she presses her nose against mine wonderingly,
but more often Lilly attacks my ankles with sheathed claws,
then somersaults onto her back to gaze at me upside down.
I can no longer leave drawers open or pens lying about.
My bathroom is smudged with paw prints.
Last night on the bus, I remembered
she was waiting for me at the front door, this hellion,
and my heart laughed.

GOOD WATER

From my window, the top-half of three elm trees,
stripped bare in December
or singing green in July,
sway and touch and talk to one another.
In big wind, they dip low and shake their great manes
like magnificent beasts. I have loved these trees
for years, and wonder if they can sense this,
wonder how potent love really is,
if it can alter a molecule's structure as some claim.
I would not alter a thing about my elms
but would like them to drink the good water of my gratitude.
Through loneliness that tore me in two
one long green summer evening,
I watched them whispering to and caressing one another,
and knew they were touching me as tenderly.

MEN DIDN'T JUST

Men didn't just lob judgments about my body
as I walked through public spaces at sixteen years old,
twenty-five, forty, they hurled them like rocks.
I endured nothing special, I'm a woman
who grew up in an America where it was OK for males
to comment on a girl's breasts and legs and buttocks, to tell her
what sexual acts they wanted her to perform on them.
Men said these things repeatedly on city streets, in town squares,
on campuses. In daytime. Loudly. With other men laughing.
And their voices were devoid of desire,
they held only aggression and anger and a will to humiliate.
It was only words, a man said to me once, as if
words didn't strike harder than weapons. As if
a man could begin to understand.
I think of this one slight body I have that engendered,
just by existing, so much male rage.
And my god, so much fear.

NOT GETTING A FELLOWSHIP

I dropped my lucky coin
into a dumpster last night.
Went into the apartment
and drank red wine and cried.

Woke up with swollen eyes
and coolness towards Marc,
as if it were *his* fault.

Sky's marbled with white today,
and from the branch of a leafless tree
a crow flings obscenities at me,
furious over the lunch I'm not sharing.

But it's nice on this bench
in sun and almost spring.
One hand on a gusty napkin.
A sandwich. Green grapes.

SATURDAY, BOOM ISLAND PARK

on the Mississippi

February   sixty degrees

skateboards   couples   bikes

A small boy   explains to his mother   while twirling

that he will put on his socks

but not his shoes

A young woman poses her dogs   one black one white

for a photo

the white dog is young

and leaps with astonished joy   at every passing stranger

Again and again   the young woman sits him dow

Her gentle voice

sings the sweet blue

of this hour

I NEVER LEARNED TO DANCE WITH A MAN

I never learned the feel of a man's hand
lightly pressing my back
or his arm encircling my waist,
rhythm and strength in his body
telling mine when to turn and to dip, assuring me
I had only to follow, the two of us so close
our warm breath might create one small cloud.
That intimacy, that grace and trust,
I never learned, and had none of the confidence
such skill might have given me as I learned about men
in other ways. And I'm not saying this is tragic,
or that my life has not been fragrant and rich
in the way it uncurled and bloomed.
I know now for instance that "mystery"
is another name for the hours we move through.
I have learned to love trees even more
than I loved them as a child. But I never learned
to dance easily with a man. If I had,
things might have been different.

THE LEPER SAID TO JESUS,
IF YOU WANT TO, YOU CAN HEAL ME

"Of course I want to! Be healed!"

I hold hard to these words,
their headlong generosity.
Never mind that for me the Gospels remain
a maelstrom of contradictions.
Certain fragments like this one
leap like glittering foam
into the blue.

Or that moment Jesus looks around angrily
(*wildly*, I imagine, his heart near-bursting)
after not one Elder would condone
his helping a disfigured man
on the Sabbath.

Or when in despair in a black garden,
he comes upon his friends sleeping peacefully
and blurts out with sudden bitterness
go ahead, sleep away!—
knowing a terrible dawn was approaching,
in shock at heaven's silence.

A REALIZATION AT 58

My life hasn't ended.

                  There will be dazzlements,

delights—

          just now, for example, my too-plump cat

is so sure of her charms

               she lolls like a mermaid

        across my bedroom's entry   in near dark,

a shadow I could easily trip over

     spilling hot tea   cursing mightily

but no,

    I note the belly she offers   with the confidence

of a great beauty

            and kneel

                and kiss it.

MORTALS AND IMMORTALS

Mortals and Immortals living in their
death, dying into each other's lives....
—Heraclitus

I think of golden-limbed gods
dying across evenings,

of muscular rivers
dying into oceans,

of buds dying into lilies
dying into longing.

What cities, what faces
do we become,

what immortals
drift through us

as we listen to rain
in unfamiliar rooms

or hesitate in dusk
though voices call.

THINKING OF TENDERNESS

It wells deep from ordinary moments
like holy water.
It may never surface in a penthouse
but seeps into the chords
of a homeless man's guitar.
Only after I left did I realize
how depleted my own relationship was
of tenderness. Years later,
he and I listened to music together
one winter afternoon. My heart was sick
over a friendship that had gone bad.
This man who knew me better than anyone
asked me what was wrong and I could not
speak, tear after tear slipped down my face.
He took my hand in his and covered it.
There was no hand I wanted more.
We had forgiven each other so much.
We seemed to float there above a still, dark pool.

WEST END GIRLS

Not Schubert or Debussy,
but a band who called themselves *The Pet Shop Boys*
wrote a piece of music that stabs
so fresh every time I hear it
I refuse to listen anymore,
although I don't have that choice in this supermarket
where they play late-80s hits nowadays.
What became of her anyway, that girl
gliding down Wells Street
in a lace tank top and miniskirt,
sweet harmonies of a British pop tune
playing in her head?
In a city that promised as much
as that song, what avenue or aisle
did she dance down
and never look back?

CHRYSANTHEMUM LEAVES

At twenty, I would not have spared this small pot
of withered chrysanthemums. At forty,
I would have breathed *thank you*
before dumping it in the trash.
Today, I snip bald heads and ruined spangles
from life that remains—
leaves that are many-fingered, like oak.
They share a sunny table with my geranium
and the cutting of aloe vera a neighbor brought over
when I moved into this garden apartment.

In my jewelry box are notes from the only man I loved,
scribbled to me on the backs of envelopes
late at night. On my walls are lilies and mermaids
painted by a sister I had hoped to grow old with.

It is easy to believe, as I climb toward sixty,
I've accomplished little, but sometimes my wealth
overflows: Bach's Suites for Lute plucked flawlessly
from a boom box. The surety a friend will call.
Leaves like green fire in morning sun.

SITTING WITH YOU

Your whole life, you almost never cried,
but you cried when you said *Death is so final.*
Quietly. Not for long. I had been telling you
what the priest and the Baptist preacher
and the women who brought you the prayer shawl told you,
that dying is a gateway, only a gateway.
After you uttered words
I had no right to correct,
I fell silent. One day, that tall tide
will roll towards me. Will *I* be fearless?

Let me take your hand now, brave girl,
and hold you safe in my memory—
sister who said words I couldn't,
sister with jade eyes, like ocean.

THE HALL YOU WALKED DOWN

The hall you walked down
stretches long in my memory
like a tunnel   a mythic passageway

Disoriented   fresh from the airport
I was not even sure it was you
this robed figure approaching
her small head
wrapped regally in a scarf

How proud you must have been
you walked the entire distance
on your own

How your fingers must have labored
over the buttons on your tunic
those defiant earrings

When at last you reached me
as if having passed
from darkness   into light
your face shone

and I   a minor character
at this scripture's edge

was speechless

SOMETIMES

Sometimes a person you love
becomes someone else. It takes years to realize
that person is never coming back.

Sometimes something wonderful occurs,
a sister you thought exotic but brittle
becomes your best friend, maybe through
mysterious and troubling circumstances. Maybe
she has a breakdown. Speaks with demons.
Walks through bright and terrible fields.

I can't know what happened inside Gale's mind
after it broke. She told me later
about the fields of lilies, the lady from Hell
who became her confidante,
but like a war veteran did not talk much
about what I could not understand.

I am trying to remember when
formality dissolved between us,
when we began to laugh together like two crones
over the same oddities. When it became easy
to tell her anything.

Sometimes I know I loved Gale enough.
Sometimes I am sure I did not.
She wouldn't agree—she believed in me more
than I ever believed in myself.

When my sister was in hospice,
I fumbled with her head scarf.
The straw I placed carefully in her mouth
dribbled water onto her neck.
I'm a bad nurse, I said,
trying to laugh away shame.

No you're not (patting my hand
with her own very weak one).
You're a good nurse.
You're a very good nurse.

MYSTERY UPON MYSTERY

But no, it is simple.
You and I stand at the corner of Willow and Morgan,
looking up at a street light's yellow globe.

Inside it, the flakes falling toward earth look different
than snow falling everywhere else in the neighborhood.

I am eight, you are twelve.
We've walked in deepening lavender for blocks and blocks,
trying to decide which house is decorated best for Christmas.

I can't see your face,
but I think that, like me,
you are almost perfectly happy.

Your body is now ashes,
yet we are standing on that corner.
Snow settles on your satin-fine hair.

WHEREVER YOU ARE

I made a spectacle of myself at the Minneapolis International Airport.
I heaved and shrieked through crowds, a middle-aged woman
burdened with coat and scarf and purse and bags,
bent on catching a plane that took off, apparently,
at the end of the world.

I'd screwed up my flight information. I realized this as I waited
calmly in line, ready to present my boarding pass,
hearing Peggy's gentle voice in my head: *If you can come, come now.*
Your sister won't be here much longer.
I realized in a sick-making flash of clarity
I had *15 minutes,*
not an hour and a half.

And went crazy.
Pushed to the front of the line without apologies.
Wept as a guard gutted the contents of my overnight bag
because of a suspicious hairbrush.
Blurted between bawls, *I'm not a fucking terrorist,*
my sister is dying!

Then ran and ran through terminal after terminal,
wild-eyed, wild-haired, sobbing, screaming

And made the flight.

My ass and my calves were sore for three weeks afterward.
You would have howled with laughter about that, Gale,
and joined me in blessing that stoic security guard
for having the humanity not to take offense.

I'm glad I made an idiot of myself for you.
I believe that, somehow, it was a gift.

THE #77 WESTBOUND

She was a Mardi Gras
on a busload of Mondays.
Just looking at her flip-flops,
the pink plastic roses
blooming between her big toes and the rest
made me feel happier.
Why buy a plain straw purse
when you can get one that grows cherries?
Why *not* wear spangles on your wrists?
I thought of the woman in double-knit pants
at the supermarket, a good-sized spray
of hyacinth in her hair:
sisters in insouciance, the two of them.
I thought of the middle-aged women
attending last night's gallery opening,
their daring reduced to earrings
purchased at arts and crafts fairs—
and how ungenerous
an assumption that was,
and how many years it had been
since I'd pinned a flower in my hair.

THE THEME WAS MEMORY

An open reading at The Writer's Place, Kansas City

You'd think a man with a poem entitled
"She Talked to the Daffodils" (dedicated
to the late Princess Diana) would be a little more humble.
You'd think he'd realize the largesse of an open mike
was the *only* reason an audience
with numbed tailbones and the despair of the polite
would listen to his very bad rhymes. Not this guy.
As thirty-some poets shared verse about memory,
he shifted like a kid in his folding chair,
clicked tongue against teeth,
tapped annoyance with a long foot encased,
that ninety-degree evening,
in battered wingtip. I know. I was sitting next to him.
He'd already flung me a dirty look
for the backpack that bulged under my chair.
This stranger in the brown woolen suit wanted
space, one of those lords who claim room for both elbows
in a movie theater. I had no idea
he was reading until the emcee called another name
and up he sprang, all twitches and angles,
muttering his way down the aisle, clutching what looked like
an entire sheaf of hand-written poems.
God help him, I thought, as, stooped over the lectern,
he recited couplets about a golden-haired beauty
who will live in our hearts for'ere. He took as his due
the astonishing sun-burst of applause. Slipped me (O me
O stunned O mortified me) a cool nod as he sat down
that said: now *that's* poetry.

BILLY RAY

Billy Ray was so cool
white boys tried to copy the way he walked
down the halls of Joliet Central
giving high fives, never breaking stride.

He was our basketball legend, Joliet's Dr. J,
who packed Will County gyms in 1972, four years
after the race riots in our town; four years
after the mayor raised Jefferson Street Bridge one night
to keep Blacks from marching to the West Side.

Billy Ray had blazing good looks and grace to spare,
the kind of grace to call a scared and skinny freshman
in third period art class "Lady Francine."
(*Lady Francine*, he said to me one morning,
you surely can draw.)

He made charm look easy as his fadeaway jump shots,
though I wonder now what Billy thought
of the football players who tried to talk jive with him,
the cheerleaders who flirted.

I wonder what happened to that super-hot kid
everyone knew would be famous one day, Billy Ray,
who was Homecoming King that year
and walked under an avenue of ROTC sabers
with a blond and beautiful Homecoming Queen
who told her friend in a cloakroom she thought was empty
how much it sucked, how she couldn't believe
she had to dance with him, too.

AT THE IVAN ALBRIGHT EXHIBIT

three girls with decadent mouths and blue-black hair
giggle nervously before *Into the World*
There Came a Soul Named Ida.
The loveliest murmurs something in Spanish
to the other two, who shake their heads.
Maybe she's just told them
what the panel beside the painting says:
that Albright's model for Ida—
mended hose sagging over varicose veins,
haggard eyes searching into a cheap mirror—
was twenty years old.

I've read he enjoyed illustrating operations
for surgeons, blending watercolors to exact tints
of sliced brain and crusting marrow;
that he had a good marriage
and was sweetly tempered.
"Corrugated mush"
was how he happened to see flesh.
Friends found him strangely childlike.

Everywhere I look, canvases bubble and writhe,
an occasional hand or startled eyeball
leaping out from the rot.
Standing in front of *Poor Room*,
whose title continues: *there is no time, no end,*
no today, no yesterday, no tomorrow,
only the forever and forever and forever without end,
a distinguished looking man in an impeccable gray suit
squeezes his wife's arm.
"Jesus, I need a drink," he mutters.

I feel my lips curling into a grin.
It'll be cold walking home,
Lake Michigan white-capped and boisterous.

ACROSS TIME AND DEATH

The yellow stain spread across blue-striped ticking
as if it had a life of its own. My sister sobbed in a corner.
It felt strange to have our bedroom light shining brightly
that dark, buried hour of the night,
but my mother's voice was soothing and low
and my father's, which daily grew tense with irritation,
held only kindness. Neither of them, woken from dead-deep sleep
after long hours of work and six kids to care for,
was the least bit angry. They turned over the mattress,
laid down clean rough sheets, tucked us back into bed.

Let me dwell on this scene when I'm tempted to finger
some distant hurt they caused, for even in middle age,
pain from childhood thrives greedily if given nourishment.
Let me cradle the seed of this long-ago night to remember
the goodness of these two people, and to tell them out loud
across time and death and the imperfect understanding
that stains every human relationship:
I thank you, I honor you, I love you.

AFTER THEY WATCHED THE *JIMMY SWAGGART TELECAST*

It was June and our late afternoon kitchen
was golden as Eden, and me tanned in cut-offs and a halter,
proud of the tossed salad I had just made for supper,
crisp vegetables glistening in the big wooden bowl.

I was bending over to pull rolls from the oven
when I felt his gaze stroking my body. The pastor.
My father's friend. The *Praise the Lord, Jesus come,
Halleluiah* man. Our eyes met; I looked away,
ashamed suddenly to be barefoot.

I was fifteen, more naïve than I realized,
but in that darker moment,
I knew I knew more about this man
than my father ever would.

WATCHING THE INTERVIEW

They were childless, they said, but loved children
even more for their loss. They had the slumped shoulders
and domed bellies of the elderly,
reminded me more of brother and sister
than husband and wife.
A dachshund slept on the man's lap.
A crocheted coverlet was spread on the couch behind them.

The video tapes—hundreds of them
found in the basement—were shocking, they agreed.
Either someone had planted them
in this bungalow where they'd lived for forty-two years,
or one of them had signed for the boxes
not realizing what was inside,
for they loved children! They loved their little dog.
This was all a terrible misunderstanding.

I remember the way they sat
like obedient students, their eyes
pleading into the camera, wistful
as a puppy dog's caught doing something wrong.
Pity us, those eyes begged, *we're not bad.*
The children were not hurt. Not really.

WORDS MEANT TO WOUND

He did not wake
as I slipped on my jeans and jacket,
closed the front door
with elaborate care.

Red leaves
by this lake I have walked to,
trying hard to out-walk
last night's words—

Red leaves
burning through mist
scorching nothing.

I let fall fill my lungs.
Study an oak leaf
as if I could learn something
from its beautiful dying.

FOR MATTHEW, WHO WILL NOT
REMEMBER ME

This is for brown-eyed Matthew
who asks excellent questions.
I know, because I sat across from him on a number 6 bus
as it inched down Hennepin Avenue
one slippery winter morning in Minneapolis.
Does that man who's sleeping in the back
have a bed, Mom?
Why aren't we wearing seatbelts?
What is a henpen?
I liked the affectionate but absentminded way
he'd lean over to plant a wet kiss on his baby sister,
gurgling in his mother's lap,
before resuming his conversation.
Why do dollar bills smell funny?
When's the next stop?
Who made the snow, Mom?
Mom.
Who made the snow?
I liked his mother, who jounced the baby and smiled,
but looked exhausted,
and how Matthew didn't fret at her silence,
but turned around in his seat and knelt
with his face pressed against the window,
staring at thick, lacy flakes
transforming the neighborhood into a Christmas globe.
Who made you, snow, he asked again quietly.
Then, after listening
to what might have been an answer,
Matthew began to hum.

IN A PARKING LOT

She had roan-colored hair and long legs.
She had been crying. I've seen, on TV, a horse whisperer
gentle a colt, slipping his rope over the animal's neck
while murmuring soothing patter, so the untamed beauty
barely notices he is now tethered. The man gentling
this woman reminded me of that, but his grip on her arm
was too tight, and she looked like she wanted to bolt
every time they reached the end of his self-ordained path.
He'd turn her around and steer her in the opposite
direction, pressing his mouth against her ear, talking, talking.
She'd been crying, but I saw wild anger in her face too
as I watched them from yards away. Neither noticed me.
Something was wrong. He held her too tight.
She was beautiful in slender jeans and that
silky auburn hair. I imagined him telling her that,
saying over and over again, *you're beautiful, babe,*
you belong to me. You're mine.

WORKSHOP

The big-shouldered woman
with the red face and work boots
brings a sonnet about her mother,
graceful and clear
as a bowl of water.

The fairy-like blond
serves up details about her marriage
in merciless couplets.

The instructor who ought to be shell-shocked,
judging from the violence of his book's imagery,
is cheerful and chatty
and offers potato chips.

None the wiser for truth,
I step into night after class
clutching groundless assumptions,

taking for granted that the moon rising
above JoJo's Bar & Grill
isn't nursing a few secrets about me,

that the man who just passed
wearing a harlequin's tights and cap
is merely an eccentric,
not a lost scrap
from someone's abandoned poem.

BEFORE SOLDIERS SHOT ANA

*During Guatemala's civil war, right-wing, military-
backed soldiers often forced civilians to witness
the executions of guerilla prisoners as a means of
intimidation.*

Her legs moved, she did not will them.
Everything she was fell away from her
like water falling from a waterwheel,
turning and weeping,
as she walked towards the woman.
Sixteen years fell away.

What remained felt the wildness
of her mother grabbing her shoulders, and the little sister
she had scolded this morning
over something, spilled oil, a broken cup,
wrapping fingers around her thighs, trying to pull
Ana back into safety, away from the men aiming rifles
at prisoners in the dusty square,
away from the woman
whose breasts bled from cuts.

Her legs moved, she did not order her body
to dismiss frantic love,
it fell away from her,
turning and weeping,
as she walked towards the uniforms
and the woman with mutilated breasts
who was looking at her now,
pleading with her to go back.

But the girl who flirted and sassed
and swore to her Momma
that one pair of American jeans
would make her forever happy
did not obey.
She had been told the stories.
She thought she knew what these soldiers
were capable of.

Her legs kept moving forward,
her life fell away from her as she
stood in front of the woman.
Touched her face.
Knelt before her.

Their weeping was the only sound
in a hushed world.

MISS NELSON

By the time I got Miss Nelson for fifth period freshman English,
she had taught at our public high school for nearly forty years.
Proud Republican, conservative Baptist,
Miss Nelson wore pumps and mid-calf pleated skirts
as she guided fourteen-year-olds through the unfamiliar waters
of Dickens and Longfellow and Shakespeare.
Easy to think of this trim gray woman
as a figurine one could place inside a box
and write on its lid in neat letters: no surprises.
But what book were we studying when a boy in class
mentioned "the Battle of Wounded Knee"
and our teacher's reaction snapped sleepy afternoon air
into something electric?
That was no battle, Daniel. It was a massacre.
Make no mistake, class. A massacre.
This in 1972, when we still swallowed
our history books whole, and were in awe of John Wayne's West.
Who knows what mighty currents rippled beneath the surface
of Ada Nelson's steady blue gaze.

HEARING MARK'S POEM ON *THE WRITER'S ALMANAC*

Old mentor. Old friend.
For too long I have thought of you
only in passing, and then not always with warmth.
I remember your old-fashioned courtliness,
but also how a precisely chosen phrase slipped into
supposedly casual conversation
could wound. Before your death,
you were estranged from two in our writing group.
For years, twice monthly, the four of us met.
Those meetings were my school, my foundation,
when I was ignorant and raw
and burned hot with love for poetry.
Now I neglect it. Now I glance at pieces
in the usual journals that receive the usual awards
and am too bored to finish them.
But today I selected one of your books
and began reading. Each poem was a door
I entered easily. You escorted me through
thought-gardens, abandoned cities,
a smoky neighborhood pulsing with
Rilke's "two more golden days."
And not only beauty, but a childhood
laced with grief, love spiked with rancor.
You gave me leave to explore your imperfect heart
and with deep pleasure, I did. And so, I hope,
will readers years from now.
They will travel with trust
through real worlds you crafted
out of fog and hand-mirrors, out of mere words—
but words chosen with a poet's precision:
alive and trembling. Perilous.

IF YOU ARE HURTING

I wish I could comfort you.
I wish I could promise you
your loved ones are waiting for you,
that the Garden is real.
I know only what my heart cries out for,
and that our lives are layered with mystery.
Today here in Minnesota, it was blue-skied
and lush and green: *beautiful,*
you and I would say. It took me six decades
to see *beautiful* in aging faces.
It took working in a nursing home,
a job I never anticipated a year ago.
I wish you could meet Lorraine, who is soft and gentle
as the petals of a violet. "I'm going outside
to visit with my mother," she told me this afternoon
with calm joy, looking illuminated from within.
I glanced out the front door, half believing
the breeze carried her mother's silvery ghost.
Or maybe a blessing.

FAITH

His smile beautifully deepens
the many wrinkles in his face. He
leans low on his walker.
He has come to the shelter today
to adopt a kitten.

COURAGE

Carefully teased auburn cannot hide
her scalp. It's not chemo, just the mean luck
of female balding. She cracks jokes with the customers
in her checkout line. Wears big earrings,
hot pink leggings.

DELIGHT

Ilse was 14 when Nazis
took over her country. Her husband of 63 years
is gone. So is her hearing.
When Ilse is not announcing to me
the scandalous doings of other nursing home residents,
her face often crinkles into joy.
Fronnie, did you see the moon last night?
A miracle! It came out of the clouds
like an angel.

LESSONS FROM SCRIPTURE

From the front desk, I hear Sandy leading Lessons from Scripture
in the TV room down the hall. She's telling the knot of residents
who attend, that although some folks believe there are many paths
to Heaven, this is a dangerous notion: Jesus alone is the Truth and the Way.
Sandy explains this cheerfully. She's always very cheerful.
I guess this means Ruth, who is Jewish, will never see God,
nor will her son who visits the nursing home twice weekly,
bringing his mother the daisies and sunflowers she loves.
Nisha's working today. She wears a hijab and her smile feels like
a beam of sun on my face. She'll give Joe a shower later,
Joe whose room smells solidly of urine. Nisha will soap him gently,
humming as if to a child. She will leave this ninety-year-old man,
who seems of late to have completely lost his way,
clean and warm and clothed.

FRONT DESK, ASSISTED LIVING

Consider Rose, whose small hands are so twisted by arthritis
she can no longer hold her paintbrush for watercoloring—
how grateful she is when I address cards for her.

Or Maria, who tells me what a wonderful life
she has had, how with so many blessings
she should accept her failing vision more cheerfully.

Or Art, who compliments me every morning on how well
I secure newspaper to those wooden poles libraries still use
("better than the weekend gals!") then declares from his wheelchair
what a fine day it is.

I've had jobs that paid more but ransacked wellbeing.
When I enter this building, I enter riches.

Consider Edna, who wheeled herself to my desk
with trembling lips and told me life was a mess, everything was a mess
because she and her only brother had just quarreled … how we hugged
and I started crying too, and we both blew our noses too loud
then laughed shakily through tears.

A YEAR AFTER GEORGE FLOYD'S MURDER

I offered so little,
just a tentative smile—

and for that, saw
what seemed weariness and distrust
fall away from her face.

She was beautiful then,
this brown-skinned woman
smiling back at a white woman
from her small front yard.

I was on my way to the corner store
for corn chips and box wine
I planned to sip over ice that evening.

Pink peonies were blooming.
It was easy to think
it could all be this easy.

HIDDEN BEACH

Today I drank deeply of blue sky and glittering cottonwoods,
of lake-freshened breezes and the buzz of fat bumblebees.
Today sun cupped my face like a warm palm.
Beauty was everywhere and I thanked God
even as I remembered the wildfires out west,
wreckage of a hurricane in Louisiana,
floods in the northeast, subways half-filled
with the Atlantic.
And that couple with the toddler.
How the terrified mother called a neighbor
from her cell phone. How they found the bodies later,
trapped in their small basement apartment.
I thought of that immigrant woman clutching her child
as ice-black water rose, the merciless moment
she had to breathe ocean into her lungs
and I said out loud, *Where were You?*
How could You let this happen?
No answer except diamonds sparkling on lake water.
The certainty of beauty and the certainty
that we are all going to die, none of us knowing
if our deaths will be as ghastly
as that mother's and father's and child's.
I was glad their horror was over.
And I'll say it, I said a prayer for them
at the hour of their death, because what do I know
about time or hope. Or faith.

WHEN EVERY
SPARROW FALLS

My god is an empty cup,
a sea turned to sand,
a cave full of wind.

In a black room
in early morning,
I pray to him.

He is silent
as time
curving into itself.

In a black room
in early morning,
he watches me.

I offer my loneliness.
He sips it
and leaves.

MARY OLIVER, I BOW TO YOU

You who gave and gave and gave still more
of the beautiful.
If you ignored streams sick with toxins,
clear-cut mountainsides,
to write of one heron-graced pond,
yours was not a refusal
to see desolation.
You celebrated what your angel
charged you to celebrate.

*

It is the small story
that can break me: a mother-to-be
locked in her steel crate,
unable to turn or stretch.
Today I learned a pregnant sow,
in despair,
cries like a human.

*

Mary Oliver, I bow to you.
I need your herons. I need your clean water
and your Aprils.

But I have other poems to write.

THE KILL LINE

Two faces, one resting against the other.
The man who took the photograph,
risking prison for exposing
a hell we are supposed to ignore,
has cropped away the hell.
We can only imagine the blood pools, the solid stench.
Whinny and scream of machinery.
Feces. Hooves.
The activist's photograph holds only the faces
of two gentle beasts,
one nestling the other as if for comfort.
Although these animals are on the kill line,
you could almost call the image peaceful.
You could almost call the image beautiful.
Because it is.

RESPONSE TO A POEM I WROTE

*97% of newborn dairy calves are forcibly removed
from their mothers within the first 24 hours*

A friend of mine who listened
deeply and without judgment
to my anger and my anguish over a man
whose jailor was vodka; a friend
who was present for me in every way
after my sister died of lung cancer
and whose six-year-old granddaughter
recently had open-heart surgery

Cannot believe I could equate
human infants with newborn animals.
I understand your goal is to shock,
she begins, which amazes me,
it seems so obvious any baby is a *baby*,
a tiny being who needs his mother,
and his mother's milk,
and soft velvet sleep.

I don't say this at the restaurant
where we hug each other before sitting down.
I don't talk of windowless buildings
where newborns are separated after birth.

We sip our white wine.
My friend is stunned I could write this poem.
I am stunned it could offend her.

INSIDE THE SEED OF ETERNITY

If the pigs are stuffed so close together
that some are regularly smothered, just
toss the dead ones into a dumpster.... If
a pregnant sow has broken a leg, leave
her in her pain until the piglets are born,
then kill her because mending her leg is
not cost effective.

Inside the seed of eternity
sing mother and baby.
She covers him with strong wings,
nuzzles him with sandy tongue,
kisses him with soft lips.

Outside, in time,
humans have degraded this bond in ways
eternity cannot comprehend
and the song has become a scream.

THE BEASTS, THE BIRDS

*And they cried out with a loud voice: He
made us. My questioning with them was
my thought; and their answer was their
beauty.*

Came the time I knew their eyes
held understanding and laughter and pain.
I ate them anyway.
Knowing what was done to them
in the factories.
Knowing many turned insane or cannibalistic.
I ate them because they tasted delicious.
Then, at night, the dream:
eating flesh on a plate and realizing
the creature was still alive, her eyes
living agony.
No accusation in them.
No hatred.
Just soft agonized eyes
looking at me
asking why.

I stopped eating animals.
The nightmares ended.

ON 2ND STREET NE

It's that brief season when trees
are still bare-limbed but whispering green
for the buds clinging to nude branches.

I walk through my neighborhood,
a woman of nearly sixty
with no fresh wisdom to share,

but I must tell you that from a distance
this young tree might appear
a cloud of light green

while up close, each bud is so crisp and distinct
I could count the number of them
on every branch.

I SHOULD HAVE STAYED

I should have stayed in the sweet city park
where mallard ducks were swimming in melted snow puddles
and sun felt like love on my upturned face.
Yes, it was time to get back to my desk,
but I should have chucked responsibility for once
and let my body soak in the glory of spring.
I could have chatted longer with Hank
who gives cracked corn to all kinds of birds
and peanut butter sandwiches to squirrels.
He showed me the islet where a mother goose is nesting
and pointed out the father flying home to her.
I should have stayed in the melting-snow-puddled park.
Hank took me to where rabbits make their home under the tool shed.
At the sound of his voice, one popped up out of nowhere
and hopped over to him. He knelt on arthritic knees
and growled *Hello there* and somewhere a cardinal whistled
his three clear notes.

BARELY JUNE

I stopped short on the sidewalk
and went back to the peonies,
bowing low from last night's downpour.
I had passed them with just a glance.
Now I lifted a bedraggled blossom
to my nose, inhaling damp perfume.

Who was I to ignore pale pink peonies?
I should know by now that if I look away,
beauty may not be blooming when my gaze returns.
The lilacs have turned to rust, and orange goblets
that were poppies are now folded tissue.

It's barely June, yet waiting for me
on my doorstep this morning
was a yellow cottonwood leaf.

YES

Late June again, and long necks of tiger lilies
rise from nests of green leaves
that are slender as rushes.
Petals crowning those stems
are hungry beaks opened wide
to receive their mother, the sun.

Flowers are like birds,
and birdsong at dusk
is like water falling, so pure and so clear.

Isn't this enough, my heart used to sob
when I was twenty, and no,
and no, it never was.

But tonight, in this
ordinary neighborhood,
the world brims over.

Enlightenment—
how many millions, over centuries,
have yearned for it.

Not me.
Not here.

WOODCHUCK

The woodchuck who ambled fat and sleek
from under the back porch
into this splash of golden light
spilled between pine branches;

who a moment ago was tearing and stuffing
the brightest green leaves
into his mouth, and is now

balanced upright on his ample bottom,
paws dangling in front of his belly
like the elegant little hands they are
(and his round little ears that just twitched,
and his merry little eyes
with their glimmer of worry),

doesn't need me to complete this sentence.
Doesn't need me at all.
If these dumb human feet
swished grass, he'd immediately,
and without complaint, turn to woods,
letting brush close over him.

Oh, but I want to hold him like a baby!
I want him to love me!

THE CANADA GEESE OF LORING PARK

These fat Canada geese
have read no self-help books,
sat through no therapy,
but are more self-assured
than I will ever be.

As I step gingerly between
their green strips of poop,
dozens of gleaming black eyes regard me
with open distaste,

for I have disrupted the flock's
seamless and solemn progression
from the north end of Loring Pond
to its southern-most tip.

(And what goose or what committee of geese,
each wearing a white wimple
and ink-dipped tapering tail feathers,
ordered this change of venue?
And to what agreed-upon end?)

I venture too close to one
who hisses, his beak opened wide to reveal
two rows of tiny serrated teeth.

Others step fussily around me,
keeping careful distance,
as if my odor were questionable.

My animal-loving nature,
my eye for their folktale charm

mean nothing to these birds.

I am the babushka woman who scrubs altar steps.
They are portly bishops debating
higher dogma as they stroll past me,
hands clasped serenely behind their backs.

ON THE WAY TO WORK

O they are happy and O they are loud!—
although only a saint, I suppose, could hear their singing.
Still, what a packed choir on this pie-shaped
piece of earth surrounded by traffic,
each chorus member craning toward me with
open-mouthed elation. I've written poems
about their sort, contemplative and lyrical, years ago.
This morning I want only to say
how glad I am to see them so glad.
Tiger lilies, you are as beautiful as ever,
and I am a year older, impatient as ever
and as hungry for praise. But you're not interested
in my or in anyone's sins.
You're too busy caroling.

MESSAGE

The fawn leapt from nowhere
onto a city freeway full of cars.

It happened so fast—
slender legs, slender back
salted with white.

If it had been dark—
if I had been speeding—

Jesus what a world we live in,
I half-sobbed
after he bounded to safety,

and I won't tell you
I heard anything
or saw words written across clouds

but a note unfolded
inside my brain

and it read
be kind.

THEIR ANSWER

Last April, we were blessed
with the usual amazement:
pebble-hard seeds
quietly breaking open
to spill glory.

But crocus and lilacs
have long turned brown.

What blooms in this
later season
is sound:
the pulsing and rasping,
cheeping and chirruping
of grasshoppers, cicadas,
tens of thousands
of fiercely alive beings.

They sob life.
They sob urgency.
A silent season is coming.

Their answer to this
is another kind of glory.
They die singing.

THE BUS SHELTER AT LAKE AND FRANCE

People leave things here:
crushed Marlboro packs, monster-sized plastic tumblers.
Today, two half-eaten doughnuts
oozing red jelly.

Stashed in a Plexiglass corner
lie remnants of an old story—
smashed Coke can, empty flask,
a purple teddy trimmed with black lace.
It's winter, and Minneapolis.
Best not to imagine.

Sometimes I throw away beer bottles
tossed near the trash bin. Sometimes I think,
yes, hell *is* other people.

This morning, ignoring the slick innards
of those two Bismarcks, I stare at a row
of scraggly bushes bordering the shelter.
On ground studded with cigarette butts,
a white-tailed rabbit
hops hesitantly among them.

He's perfect.

CAT GARDEN

I adopted him out of grief
after losing my Lillybird (her golden eyelashes,
her sweet-smelling tummy!)
but this morning, my wild new boy
of white boot and bib
turned from the window's enticements
to smile at me

and a seed took root.

TRANSFIGURATION IN NORTH MINNEAPOLIS

Blinding white, the sudden wings beat
in front of my windshield, as if
the gull had dropped from a horizon
of sapphire sea and chalk-bright cliff
instead of this dreary March sky
hanging low over a parking lot edged
with a Dollar Tree, a Taco Bell,
black-crusted snow.

I watched him ascend, dazzling white,
such as no fuller on earth could bleach....
wings that might have flown straight from the womb
of the first day.

TO THE HAWK ON THE WINDOW LEDGE

You came.
And like a white flower
belief opened.
You were close enough to touch
and stayed long seconds   (I hardly dared
breathe).

I may stumble through wrong decisions,
make my way down the lesser road—
I will still be blessed.
(Your feathers ragged from northern winters,
your presence austere.)

You left, tearing
longing from me.
Carrying it with you.

VOCATIONS

The Man of the Year plays
with rockets and empires,
wants to blast
tunnels under Asia, build
high-rises on Mars.
Me, I'd be happy to make you see
what I saw this morning:
a piece of black cloth carried
this way, that way, by wind,
sinking gradually earthward
to drape itself on a pine branch,
shake out irate feathers,
become Crow.

EVEN THE MOON

I'm walking through an October day so glorious
even the moon wants to partake of it,
her ghost-like white disk gazing serenely from rich blue.
The world's bronze, burnt orange, scarlet,
and I've paused by a little tree with round leaves that resemble
pale yellow coins. Such wealth.
I was raised with religion. Sometimes it helped me,
sometimes it damaged, but gold leaves and blue air
never did anything but help. And words sometimes….
In my heart of hearts, God is closer to me
than I am to myself. I read that quote
by Augustine this morning, and salt water welled.
Imagine a Creator who loves us like that. Impossible.
So are these pale yellow coins.
So is this priceless day.

WILD MARE

Poems may come again, maybe not.
Meanwhile, I want to tell you my young cat
has astonished eyes the exact green
of a bottle of ginger ale,
and my heart gallops on with fury
and sorrow and repentance and wonder.
How did I ever become 63 years old.

NOTES

"Response to a Poem I Wrote"—italicized quote is from "Ten Dairy Facts the Industry Doesn't Want You to Know," freefromharm.org

"Inside the Seed of Eternity"—italicized quote is from the essay, "Are We Addicted to the Suffering of Animals?" by John Berkman (the author deplores the practices he names here).

"The Beasts, The Birds"—italicized quote is from *St. Augustine's Confessions*, Book X.

WITH LOVE AND GRATITUDE

Thank you to Marge Barrett and Ricky Peterson, beloved fellow writers, for your insightful feedback and suggestions. You both make me a better writer.

Thank you to Marcy Darin, Genie Lerch-Davis and Maureen Perkins for your wonderful friendship and support. I am lucky to have you in my life.

Blessings to Marcie Wollesen who has been, from the budding of our friendship, a Guardian Angel to me.

I am grateful for all of my five sisters. Katherine, especially, has championed my writing. Gale was my dearest friend in the world.

Finally, thank you, Marc Marcovitz. My Marco. My rock.

ABOUT THE AUTHOR

FRANCINE MARIE TOLF's poems and essays have been published widely in journals both local and national. She has received two Minnesota State Arts Board Grants and grants from the Elizabeth George and Barbara Deming Foundations. Francine lives and works in Minneapolis.

www.ingramcontent.com/pod-product-compliance
Lightning Source LLC
Chambersburg PA
CBHW031005090426
42737CB00008B/681